MAPMAKING

MAPMAKING

Megan Harlan

Winner of the John Ciardi Prize for poetry.
Selected by Sidney Wade.

 BkMk Press
University of Missouri-Kansas City

BkMk Press
University of Missouri-Kansas City
5101 Rockhill Road
Kansas City, Missouri 64110
(816) 235-2558 (voice)
(816) 235-2611 (fax)
www.umkc.edu/bkmk

Cover Art: Michael Smith
Title Type: Kara Davison
Author Photo: Matthew Culligan
Book design: Susan L. Schurman & Michael Smith
Managing Editor: Ben Furnish
Associate Editor: Michelle Boisseau
Editorial Assistant: Elizabeth Gromling
BkMk Press wishes to thank Curtis Bauer, Lindsey Martin-Bowen,
Susan Cobin, Greg Field, Steve Gehrke, Elaine K. Lally, Andrés Rodríguez,
Maryfrances Wagner, and Karen I. Johnson
Printing by McNaughton & Gunn, Saline, Michigan.

Previous winners of the John Ciardi Prize for Poetry: *Tongue of War* by Tony
Barnstone, selected by B.H. Fairchild; *Black Tupelo Country* by Doug Ramspeck,
selected by Leslie Adrienne Miller; *Airs & Voices* by Paula Bonnell, selected by
Mark Jarman; *Wayne's College of Beauty* by David Swanger, selected by Colleen J.
McElroy; *The Portable Famine* by Rane Arroyo, selected by Robin Becker; *Fence
Line* by Curtis Bauer, selected by Christopher Buckley; *Escape Artist* by Terry
Blackhawk, selected by Molly Peacock; *Kentucky Swami* by Tim Skeen, selected
by Michael Burns; *The Resurrection Machine* by Steve Gehrke, selected by Miller
Williams

Library of Congress Cataloging-in-Publication Data

Harlan, Megan.
  Mapmaking / Megan Harlan.
    p. cm.
  "Winner of the John Ciardi Prize for poetry, selected by Sidney Wade."
  ISBN 978-1-886157-77-4 (pbk. : alk. paper)
  I. Title.
  PS3608.A7438M37 2010
  811'.6--dc22

                    2010036657

This book is set in Garamond.

ACKNOWLEDGMENTS

Grateful acknowledgment to the editors of the following journals for originally publishing these poems:

AGNI Online, "Ex Libris"

Arts & Letters, "Monumental" and "Stained Glass"

The American Poetry Review, "Nativity"

Bellingham Review, "Land of the Lotus-Eaters"

Beloit Poetry Journal, "Living Cloisters" (reprinted on *Poetry Daily*)

Columbia Poetry Review, "Slower"

Cairn, "Transparency"

Hayden's Ferry Review, "Ocean Elegy" and "Animal Instinct"

The Laurel Review, "The Marvelous Plague"

Meridian, "City Garden" (reprinted on *Poetry Daily*)

Natural Bridge, "Clare Island"

New Orleans Review, "Museum of Natural History"

Nimrod International Journal, "Inhabited"

Notre Dame Review, "Mother Tongue," "Mother Wit,"
        "Motherhouse, " "Puppet Theater," "The World"

Phoebe, "Atget's Paris" and "The Blue Ballet"

Prairie Schooner, "Caravansary" and "California"

Puerto del Sol, "Rendezvous in Exile"

Sycamore Review, "Motel Limbo"

TriQuarterly, "Farsickness" and "Multiverse"

Special thanks to *Poetry Daily* for republishing "City Garden" and "Living Cloisters." My heartfelt thanks to Sidney Wade for choosing my manuscript, and to Ben Furnish, Michelle Boisseau, Michael Smith, Susan Schurman, Kara Davison, and BkMk Press for their generous and thoughtful work on my book. I am grateful for the inspiration of my former writing teachers and classmates, and to my family and friends for their support, especially Marni Ayers, Evan Harlan, and my mother, Sherry Harlan. Above all thanks to Matthew Culligan, for his love, belief, and encouragement.

MAPMAKING

I.

II.

III.

IV

FOREWORD

The poems in this book exhibit Megan Harlan's great attention to and skill with form, sound, and language. The poems are constantly surprising, taking us to the far corners of the poet's metaphorical maps, and, in her words, "gesturing us to go further." This is imaginative writing at its very best—visual, aural, metaphorical, ethical, and adventurous. The poet constructs genuinely new topographies for us that offer significant and original inroads into our understanding of what it means to be human.

—Sidney Wade
Final Judge, John Ciardi Prize for Poetry

For my mother, in memory of my father,
and for Matthew, always.

I

EX LIBRIS

Here is the fossil as a perfume. Here is a bone
picked clean and whittled into a tiny tall ship.
Here are magicians teaching secrets
to contortionists. Here is colored glass on fire.
Here is love broken into vowels and a shrug.
Here is scripture forged into the memory of water.
Here are rosettes, exposed wiring, teasings onto the brink.
Here is the full vista of an hour, and the sun.

FARSICKNESS

rough translation of *fernweh (Ger.)*:
the opposite of homesickness.

Imagine a love turned out
as bread best cast

to the rivers, feedings
for smaller, far-flung things—

fire-flights of stillness,
forms alighting, then airborne,

until the breeze begins
to feel like hunger,

the wayward sweep of desire—
for the holy wheel

rotating foot, breath, and earth,
the pilgrim's chaff,

frayed and heliocentric,
in need of distance

as a horizon of prayer
to both call and receive.

MULTIVERSE

They say stories should hold their shape.
But the city metabolized my stories whole,

floodlit them for flaws and rare alleles,
disposed of the cell walls, released their codes

and inner logic to the streets. Returned one for a song,
in a basement bar, two months later—through a guitar

chord's red-glazed order—as I saw how it,
that love, cut even closer. Another on the E train

when I forgot my stop because
an old man beamingly called me "Lucy," wanted

to know how Charlie was doing, and for an instant
how I wanted to tell him. Hey, I'm walking here

too. The way these scripts move underfoot,
the streets strewn with newspaper stories

on city life, a foliage of tiny, half-read chatter.
They've got columns and columns to fill,

Romes of text built and razed every day—
like poetry ripped from the line

and ruthlessly hacked for another cup of coffee.
Try to find a greater New York novel.

The sick, homeless boy who lived on my corner
was always thumbing through—no joke—

Les Misérables, and accepted my change for his vignettes
of revolution and metropolis. One day

he disappeared. Just like what? They say stories
should answer why, the linear sequence engraving

sense. But throw in that extra dimension—
the cast of thousands I called home—

and the permeable membrane becomes
the only line worth mentioning. That, and the

cross street. What passes through in tendrils—
Urdu, trash-talk, creamy fine-dining patter—

may take root, die off, collide spectacularly within
to tear free a whole new system,

the way the beefy security guy whispered to me
as I left the bank that wretched afternoon,

"Some days are better than others." That was it.
But like magic the cave door creaked open.

CITY GARDEN

After the restaurant, the miracle grew
so large we bought more wine,
took each other to bed. Outside, blocks of time
drifted from the traffic lights, and the ending

could not be told over the bus-brakes,
drunks and children wailing from the streets.
As in any famous city, we could see no stars.
Astrology abandons us in times of excellence

and mischief. My best guess at forever
was the planter on the windowsill, filled
with store-bought herbs and soil, Miracle-Gro
like a firmament of shameless chemical stars.

MAPMAKING

The vessels of ink,
planes of canvas

returning the last
frontiers, those rich,

geodesic kingdoms
of *you are here*

flayed and crushed
to scale, the human,

cardinal syntax of
forests and tunnels

hide-outing wasteland,
fear, the flux wondered

into colors coded
for wilderness, interchange,

routes chosen for what they
bypass, pigments hustled

by trade winds, overland,
quick approximation

on a restaurant napkin,
land-masses torn

like fabric, spliced
into current fashion,

the precise whereabouts
of plazas where time

feels circumscribed, mere
sculptures of twilight,

sunrise, hints of earth's
curvature revealing where

we each go missing,
each arrived in a place

entering skyward,
gesturing us to go further.

NATIVITY

My family is a shore never reached.
My family is supernatural,
like a primitive legend, or higher math.
My family crops up in historical tales.
My family is a scent I can't detect.
My family is a lissome direct object.
My family likes the chase.
My family favors the edges of continents.
My family is laid to waste—
and all of our reasons.
My family is an occasional sense of mission.
My family is the tidal rhythm of conversation.
My family is always moving—in pulse rates,
dreaminess, a taste for salt. It won't keep still.
My family is an abandoned sanctuary.
My family looms in my periphery.
My family collects pretty stones on walks.
My family is a study in metabolic contrasts.
My family can't escape without looking back.
My family appears in hundreds of photos
I don't know what to do with.
My family rakes it in. My family loses it all.
My family is a form of logic
based on bucking up and bearing down.
My family lapses into silence.
My family prefers Scotch.
My family wanders like lambs
through the empire's domain.
My family doesn't fall sway.
My family is beyond belief.
My family sleeps soundly
and spends the morning in pajamas.

My family sticks to its guns.
My family is a dialectics of rhyme and reason.
My family becomes an all too common tragedy.
My family at this moment shows love.
My family is used. My family shines through.
My family holds me in its arms. My family lets me go.

MONUMENTAL

Mountain View Cemetery, Oakland, California,
designed by Frederick Law Olmstead in 1863

Imagine the soft borders of this walled city, drifting beyond
the parking and stone pines, the pyramids, pagodas, and obelisks

the size of shrubs, crypts with columns or Gothic spires
strewn with calla lilies and beer cans, their shrunken architecture

of unlived future, forevers collapsed into memory and stone.
I am enormous, five days past due, breathing hard, my son

folded neat as a ribbon within me. Even the mourners stare.
I hike hills curtained with visions of water and bridges

and hand-sized metropolis—Oakland's port of freights beneath
San Francisco's soft-shell domes, from here a floating parable

of fortunes told—sifting behind cherubs and Celtic crosses,
stars of David and fleurs-de-lys, headstones cascading these slopes

with the hieroglyphs of birth and death, each marker a blind
door to the classic arc of story, stark as professions of love.

At a simple plot, a man plants a silver pinwheel, and the breeze
sends it spinning—the flutter and spark like an invitation to thin

air, whatever borderland encrypts the invisible with ornaments,
fertile-smelling shirrs of eucalyptus leaves swaying over me, the man,

the woman walking her dog who calls to me, "Any minute now."
My belly is a public unveiling. We have settled on a name

and in this landscape names are the voices in the cathedral,
the object lesson of the chant, the dialect where the legend

begins and ends by heart. Our Johnny and Dearest Rebecca
line the old stone path to wild saffron poppies, a sprinkler casting

prismatic sizzle into the earth. Today I could believe we are always
in conversation with that other world—where disappearance

becomes paradise, time held aloft by wish, abyss, and an etiquette
of flowers—at a frequency too high or deep to decipher, our bodies

caught in common, glorious light. "The good don't die," proclaims
the epitaph for a seventeen year-old girl, ninety-four years dead. But,

they do. My son is a day away from this universe that will replace me
as his atmosphere. It's called a miracle, as if we are absent from it.

But how it feels is the way the sky blasts the reflecting pool
blue and white, swirls with the tidal sound of traffic, destination

as speeding shine and particulate. Or the way my husband takes
my hand as we pass the columbarium, talk a little of my father's ashes,

who knows where, the minutes devouring me into an entryway
to my own buried home, a place windowed with renaissance.

ATGET'S PARIS

Eugène Atget, 1857-1927, documentary photographer of Paris.

We are partially noticed. Black shudder of balustrade, piles condemned
for soft medieval bones. Daylight a woven gone, as if the visible

planets could worry themselves into a basket of flowers, a store front
      of dolls,
each still, bare alley a constellation of angle and stone. A garden chair
      fallen

below memory, swarming leaves. The blasted coordinates of afternoon,
ironwork, bed clothes, staircase, all directives past our sense of loss,

the sheer elsewhere, the structure of shining, airless white within
      each frame.
The boulevards unburdened of motion, shadowing chaos, even

the rag-and-bone men posed and waxen. Somewhere, the living
      memory
lies in wait. The makeshift city flutters past another hour. The genius

becomes the statue, the cobblestone. The beauty that will not save us
pools and shimmers, invocatory. It is a category of worn street-signs.

II

THE WORLD

Do you believe in ghosts? One night,
I went to The World, a club deep
in Alphabet City. As I danced with my friend,
a young man there was shot dead.

A different night, a few blocks away,
I dreamt my father visited me.
I ran into him on a brilliant city street.
Picture a New York gone infinite,

a little pearly. We hugged, amazed at
our meeting, and then went to eat
at a sidewalk café. I kept grabbing his arm,
so happy, asking: Are you real?

He laughed at this, his presence.
The next morning, I got the call saying
he'd been found dead, far from me.
What part of the world had I seen?

Maybe you know of this sort of thing,
or have your doubts. The first time
I visited New York I went to The World.
I last saw my father in the real world

at the corner of West 4th and West 11th,
which somehow cross, like a bend in the continuum.
He was getting into a cab to catch a plane.
I knew deep inside how it would end.

And when the call came, the walls,
they did close in. It's the world that moves
in mysterious ways, I've found. Or as my brother
later said of my dream, "At least

we know he's okay, wherever he is."
Not that we believe in ghosts. Yet I took
my father's arm, we sat in those chairs.
The world visited us somewhere.

MUSEUM OF NATURAL HISTORY

I was too old to hold my father's hand.
We walked through the long galleries,

past exhibits I don't remember.
But I still imagine the marble floors,

the musty dioramas of Early Man,
the many exits through doors marked

emergency. These open like chutes
through evolution, the fires, earthquakes,

other hells. And in between flourish signs
describing knowledge as a flattened surface,

as if it could be, a herding together
of teeth and shards and basketry,

an inquisition of the normal as it stems
from nameless appetites. We pretend

to name them, the urge to pierce feathers,
one by one, to create a dodo's replica,

or an afternoon spent gazing at white
suspended whale bones that fill the air

like angels held accountable for
our every abandonment.

LAND OF THE LOTUS-EATERS

Take a perfect form and feed it flattery.
Take a choir that sings, *I don't want to preach.*
March a child through seasons of glass
breaking. Take an island of infinite doors.
Take fruit rotting to musical pulses,
tokens for passage, embedded in leaves.
Strain the structure of home through a sieve.
Hold the doors to the continents drifting,
air and waves lapping, monuments basking.
Your journey is like a bell ringing.
Bury nothing. Believe what you will.
Take an island that no one remembers.
Take a choir that sings, *Not without a fight.*
This place is your longing, drowning in light.

TRANSPARENCY

Morning, buoyant as a lotus, stemless flower.
It feeds on air and liquids, shifting elements:
Memory drowned in milk,
the you who is deep and missing.

Many times, the sky folded me into itself.
Flying that high up, drifting off,
I felt transparent as a feather veined apart.
The horizon out the window was a stem

of air and water. Nowhere moving higher.
In this whiteness, birds formed patterns.
The you I want cannot be asked for.
I drift in and out of answers.

STAINED GLASS

I stopped inside a church
in midtown for a few minutes,
its prolific gifts
collected over centuries
for someone else.
I have a fixed idea of life.
I often suspect it's entirely wrong.
It is solid as a building,
indoors on a beautiful day.
In a painted sky are creatures
with wings but no souls,
though how can we tell.
The soul is not body or stone.
The soul is an emptiness,
maybe filled with something
we can't see, like time,
time buried alive.
Our bodies forgive it, helplessly.
This emptiness also resembles
doubt. This emptiness resembles
the soaring air inside the church—
the shape of time as beauty,
or doubt as passion—
but I am literal-minded,
a story spent in flight,
like the stained glass windows
radiant with midtown.

SIERRA LAKE

To invent from the nested rhythm of trees
a memory. In the lit drafts of needles and pollen
you're with me again, in the guiltless sun
over granite stones smelling of silver and clay,
our words bright as coins thrown in a fountain.
To near the lake, to see how it contained
reflected drifts of cliff, cloud, and green,
surges of shade towing blue, directionless archways.
And when we dove in, we swam through
a winter poured free of its glacial heart.

ISLAND OF APPLES

the island of the afterlife in Welsh mythology

Where do I see him—
in a kind of field worn open
at the center, as if nothingness

was an entry without end.
An atmosphere gone cold, then
brighter, bolder,

a story without people.
It tells how what once existed
has now healed.

Myths rise like fabrics of light,
tethered to actual place—
the only love without degree.

There must be a boat, and a sea,
an end to the burning.
And a way to find the shore.

MOTEL LIMBO

Say, after a fall,
you could not remake yourself
in your own image:
An electric vacancy,
the last room.
It's on the top floor—
an elevation of thieves
pilfering Bibles
from nightstand drawers.
It's an anonymous room
you've stayed in before,
a way-station for the displaced,
parsed of flight.
Wrapped in soiled bedding
bleached clean, you watch the TV
bolted down for a swift eternity
of tiny, quelled revolutions,
consider escape routes,
since the lock is a rattling joke.
After the long drive,
when exits flashed past you
like run red lights,
the radio mutated
through stations of the cross-
country, you consider this hiatus
a rented house arrest,
penitence for the fly-by-night—
slim paper-wrapped soaps
like calling cards left
by a literal-minded god.
Limbo is the motel room

of eternal return,
a key to a strange bed
for fitful but unquestioned rest,
a blessed respite in judgment,
machines with unlimited ice.

INHABITED

Imagine my loss of you as a city.
　　For years I wandered its streets—
through perplexing districts
　　of diamonds, gargoyles, and bodegas,
of dive bars, operas, resurrections.
　　These views passed before me
like streamers flung
　　in celebration of a new dictator,
the lock-stepped present tense.
　　It was a gift, that busy-ness,
history manufacturing only
　　crumbling bricks, those faded
gangland thoroughfares, breath
　　of old wool coats, the texture
of the place's constant excavations.
　　For my living, I learned the language
of gypsies and brokers,
　　their patter of forgiveness,
its flexible vistas.
　　I learned that the future
is not the exit from a labyrinth,
　　but a kiosk on the corner
selling maps to the city's streets
　　for pocket-change.

III

RENDEZVOUS IN EXILE

You could mistake a map for a mango.
Your signature strung like a violin.
You could peel the skin from sweet,
fibrous threads. You could leave a mark.

I've forgotten the days since then.
I've held maps like a child in my hands.
I've eaten fruit like music folded into
chambers. I've lost everything again and again.

You could tell me your name is a witness.
I could give you a map like a fruit's
edible skin. You could answer a child
with music. I could leave a mark on you.

OCEAN ELEGY

Childhood remembers itself as an ocean.
Tide swept out, the water shallow, patternless.
Whiteness foams the indigo and green.
We visit from on high, an entrance like the sun.
When we return, the entrance does not quite lead us
back to now. The light here has paled.
It is now, but cryptically patterned,
because we thought the ocean marked a start.
We thought it would lead somewhere beyond us.

ANIMAL INSTINCT

The morning's soft, shiny pelt.
A bird's worth of restlessness.
The heart clattering like hooves on glass.
Each hour's exposed, fractured teeth.

MOTHERLAND

1. Mother Cell

The inward door opens
like an oyster shell:
Lost cosmos of nacre,
flesh, and irritants,
embroidery by heat.

The weather calms;
some boats go missing.
Beneath, the months pass
like a coral reef
accreting tidal alphabets.

2. Mother Tongue

Language of ecstasy.
Language of necessity.
Language of tricky subjunctives.
A miner's lingo of salt and gold.
Creole of needle-fine irony.
Logic of second thoughts.
Lexicon of the well-timed obscenity.
Lexicon of sweet and savory.
Psalms of wool and knives.
Psalms of forgotten dances
and speechless fears.
Psalms stained with milk.
Word roots of the divine.
Body language of the divine.
Vernacular of heavy lifting.
Verb forms for continent, for fruit.
Grammar of mutable pronouns.
Language of improvisation.
Language in rapid expansion.
Pleas for precious living things.
Pleas for no one but us.
Language of unrivalled ambition.
Language of gratitude.

3. Mother Wit

For the razor's edge.
For a million white lies,
texture of snowflakes
in a melting landscape.
For mechanical elegance.
For a galloping pace.
For the reflection in facing
mirrors, kaleidoscoping
towards forever.
For the ringing like wind chimes,
carved of daily weather.
For a primeval address
in liquid and bone.
For this crystal prison,
the door swung open.
For forgiveness, a harmonic,
high-strung instrument.
For the mind's own agriculture,
grafting translucently.
For this fortune
hell-bent on discovery.

4. Mother-of-Pearl

Time set to the speed of pearls.
Mountains broken from pearls.
Pearls alighting like swans in rivers.
Pearl whirlpools, pearl mirrors.
Sky-pearls, street-pearls, sea-pearls.
Missions, congregations of pearls.
Crypt-pearls, skull-pearls.
Galactic, unbelieving pearls.
Pearls soaked in sunlight.
Pearls crushed into table wine.

5. Motherhouse

Pooled with human voices.
Built with its ruin in motion.
Built by the skin of our teeth.
Raised in palettes of ocean and earth.
This architecture of gnawing bones.
Designed in rhythmic tapestry.
Built to curl up to.
Framed with luminous flaws.
This architecture of hothouse blooms.
Built of a heaven so misunderstood.
Built like a traveling circus.
Built amid aqueous vistas.
Constructed of anachronism.
This architecture of deciduous growth.
Raised with an eye for symmetry.
Built over strong objections.
Built for climbing up and out of.
Built to be blind-sided.
Finished with sharpened edges.
This architecture alive with witness.
Built with nests of untold grief.
Built for drifting, as in cream.
Built to withstand the force
of anything that sings.

MOVING DAY

The ruins wait for my departure,
my latest counter-revolution. I am

beside myself—a thousand strangers
who left me with their papers

shed like hair, trinkets charged as dice.
I tape them up in boxes, shards of sagas

broke from former epochs, resolutions,
pieces of my history jigsawed

from old versions of the future.
In my real one they proved so unstable,

kept disintegrating into movement,
into people, the sky burial of each year.

CARAVANSARY

The day is a landscape escaping
from the earth. Every day I moved away
from you, past walls of closed doors,
through colors charting the outskirts of a life.

Imagine all the doors cast open, all the other
strangers. Travel is how love pretends
to change. A new room unlike forgiveness,
unlike the soul. A scattering of uses

for escape. Every night the center changes,
hunkers down. A chamber like the heart—
with solid walls, transfusing starlight—
fills in for love, this bed without you.

CALIFORNIA

It breaks apart into chasms and dry heat.
Freeways pierce the shore like detours to a holy site,
limned by money, tar, the scented gold
of grass and eucalyptus, cars and last resorts.

What is holier than a way to feel again,
even if by money we mean a last resort, or by beauty
we mean detour. Its inlands erupt with glaciers,
gold and avocados like bones jutting through skin,

and its skin is beauty felt as heat. Like canyon hawks,
the freeways hover over subdivisions,
and the mirror of the Pacific, gone cloudy and forgiving,
fragments endlessly from within.

IV

THE MARVELOUS PLAGUE

"The Return of the Marvelous Plague, Art in the World," Gabriel García Márquez's
1985 article in *El Tiempo*.

It moves through breeze, breath, airborne.
It moves through dream, blood, darkness.

It resembles the sticky membrane of a song,
or a fragrance so dense it might cast fine-boned shadows.

When we are struck with it, flushed
as if with a sickness lifting, the fever breaking,

our bodies are in thrall to its flavors. Who could
doubt it comes on like wildfire, downpour,

a swoon of glamour—look at all this great lighting.
It is memory turned outward, finally, released

like captive birds taking up their ancient migrations.
It is salt on the skin, the instinct to taste it.

It appears as yellow cherries on a dry summer day,
white light splayed, collapsing to color, the moment

when every wedding guest gets up and dances.
It moves as a throughway, a fluting, a seizure

of kissing, the magnitudes of our deep blue pulses,
hale and hidden as the ballet of equilibrium,

bees in a graveyard. After the time of rend,
it is the fit to return, return to the world,

supple within it, air to the stars, a literate thread,
when the glare no longer seems so bright,

the noise dies down, beloved face in a crowd,
it is meant to be spread.

CLARE ISLAND

The path I'm on rises to the sky, where blue brocades
with fleshy white and silver. I'm alone, reaching held within

its stretch. The fertile smell of water stilled on rock,
in pockets, stones strewn or in rows, an island of eyes, unseeing

as a potato's bitter sprouts. Hillsides striped with potato ridges
       abandoned
during the Famine, but tilled for centuries until permanent

as fingerprints, scar-lines deeper than their healing, a muddied script.
Their sinking rhythm pulls the land inward, backward, as if

I'm walking in a place that lived beyond its future.
It feels familiar, a burial in shifting light.

Tiny yellow orchids douse the grasses like some strange spice.
The dead, tilled lines call for a new crop,

all fields cast open for dreaming. All fullness, all hunger,
shameless for plenty. But the island is an element,

a single mountain stitched with crystals.
You can pick them up loose, milky as cakes of soap,

gardens full of clouded lenses, pieces scattered
near cliffs locked against pale Atlantic inlets, like windows

broken from the landscape, imagined whole.
Even the place-names in a language that died with the trees

become pathways that lead beyond sight: The Half-Wooded Hillside.
The Eagle's Peak. The Cave of the Starlings. The Black Garden.

They mark borders of memory, translating silence.
Bernie, a native-born farmer, opened the medieval church,

its rare pagan frescoes of dragons, peacocks and sex,
hunting in primary colors, bright as ripe fruit.

He talked of cancer rates today, from dirty milk, polluted meats.
He talked of the blight on a staple crop hailing from South America;

an island of seafarers who fled on coffin ships. To bear, yes,
their descendents, I was shy to admit, as if a place could

break itself into bone. As if I could locate its losses
with my own, fields dissolving to elsewhere, feeding

continents, storms, stars, bordered with stones, with dirt roads.
Facing the mainland are *doons*, footprints of Stone Age forts,

now just the faintest impressions of circles in grass.
What grow are palm trees and thistle, and Portuguese moss.

PUPPET THEATER

Take the story of the knight errant
and the Paladins who tricked him,

and watch it, a thousand years later,
in a velvet box filled with wooden dolls.

The story resembles a fossilized person.
The strings hold the forms erect.

Delirious costumes precede the events.
People are concealing their voices.

Admire the ribbons and gold paint
as the story continues to approximate

crimes that took ages to occur:
We killed our enemy, his children

stole our land, *etcetera*—and all its
shrewd, collapsible beauty. Tragedies

play quick strokes of the hand,
cross weapon, toy, and talisman.

Everyone peers at the stage.
How long did it take to organize

so much chaos and rage into a script
built from strangers' throats?

Since stories don't live,
they only make sense from afar.

They do not rewrite anything.
They hold the strings taut.

The room is still. The scene in the box
is busy: wood men with swords,

wood women with painted flesh.
The drama untangles curse from wish.

Now the ending is upon us.
Now the story plagiarizes grief.

Now the stage is so quiet, all
we hear in the room is our breath.

SARAAB

Saraab: Arabic for desert mirage.

I could walk forever toward you,
the vision oscillating

like the dailiness of our
love, a far oasis

tethered to my sight,
or blindness, the atmosphere

and bright, migrant spaces
we've created

casting up this paradise
real enough to photograph—

geometries of light and heat
displacing a shard of sky

into the earth,
a glassy, blue-green garden

or is it city moving parallel
with my horizon,

iris, and aperture,
what I see of you

at the edge of the day,
refracted across emptiness.

THE BLUE BALLET

A stage of touch. A heaven saved
from an anonymous night within us.
Shadows deepen, fire of the invisible,
rising amid our bodies and our pasts.

Our skin unfolds voiceless stories:
dusk walls fainting, indigo crossings.
Gestures of taming and flexure, crushes
and envy, heaven's wastelands reclaimed.

Direction bears deeper, as the past lifts
into cosmos, electricity. Our bodies left
in embrace's blue flame, muscles
with darkness and extends like flight.

THE PALMIST'S DEFENSE

You come to hear about odds
in your favor, the fix on the Lotto,
slow trysts with a beautiful stranger.

You know the skin is an organ,
a solo instrument of prints, engraved
with the wit of genetics.

I know the lines for your life and heart,
your health and fate, your money
and head, your spirit and sex

spell out the will of your ancestors,
ghost-written and read—so many
prayers for the sick, shopping lists,

scrapings of crust from the pan—
the rippling wake from two people
we refer to as *today*. You want

the secret, high adventure, magic numbers
of children and dollars. You don't
want to hear how love can bend us

beyond the recognition of our dreams,
how bravery is the fire cooling
within the burn, and common as laughter.

SLOWER

Because we are built of rest as well.
Because rest locates us, a parallel chase

to here, our bodies tamping down the earth,
ribbons of drowse and float

scrimshawing our bones. A source
overflowing of itself, a genealogy

of sleep, generations of night
skies seeping forth in scentless drifts.

And for dreams beyond the broken
shore, the bird-haunted ocean,

the nets cast down in woven waves,
beyond the capturable remains

of anything we've wanted.
Because rest fills us with moments

lifted writhing from their shells,
the gnarled, opalescent shells

we describe in vain to anyone
who'll listen, while the living flesh

we devour without a thought,
like stones falling to the ocean floor,

where they lay, forgotten in our time,
but also whole, protected,

the way sleep comes still and liquid,
and waits for us on a forgotten shore.

LIVING CLOISTERS

They raise themselves around us,
sudden shelters

within the larger outpour,
courtyards sprung

from currents of a brighter
force, palmful

of another's hand, voice
rung down the spine,

stringing archways
within a space that shapes

nothing but its own dimensions,
a rhythm without song,

a corrugated darkness
hewn to colonnades and bells

by our names, meals,
momentary vows, sanctums

opening around a fountain,
its waters illuminated

like figurated calligraphy
in a root, arterial language.

Megan Harlan lived in seventeen different homes across four continents by the time she graduated from high school. She now lives in Berkeley, California. Recently Harlan's poetry has appeared in *American Poetry Review*, *TriQuarterly*, and *Notre Dame Review*. Harlan's short stories, travel writing, and book reviews have appeared widely, including in *The New York Times*, *Alaska Quarterly Review*, *San Francisco Chronicle*, and elsewhere. She holds degrees in creative writing from NYU and Tufts. *Mapmaking* is her first book.